mel bay presents

Understanding Guitar Chord Progressions

by bob balsley

1 2 3 4 5 6 7 8 9 0

Visit us on the Web at www.melbay.com — E-mail us at email@melbay.com

Introduction

Guitarists are different from other musicians. Look in the mirror! And the guitar is very different from other instruments. My first book (*Understanding Guitar Chords–Mel Bay 1998 catalog # MB96932*) provided an easy way to see how chords are constructed from a few basic forms. This book uses the same ideas to illustrate how chords can be put together to make chord progressions.

When I first began playing guitar, my friends taught me **songs**. Later, I used my ear and experience to learn **songs** on my own. I think this is the case with most guitar players. Much later, I realized that I really didn't know what I was doing, I was just playing songs from memory. To remedy my ignorance, I wrote *Understanding Guitar Chords* and finally began to understand what I was doing when I played. To make a long story short, the more I understood, the better I played, and the better I played the more confidence I gained.

My first revelation was that every type of music from classical to country comes from the same scale, the same 12 notes, and every form of music from rock to reggae has expanded these notes to stretch our ears, challenge our brains and express our emotions.

An understanding of guitar chords will enable you to get more out of this book but regardless, we will start with some very basic stuff. There will also be *Playbreaks* in notation and tablature of progressions and songs to provide some concrete examples. Join me on a logical and whimsical journey as "Louie, Louie" evolves into the blues and beyond.

Understanding Guitar Chord Progressions

Table of Contents

Louiex2, Sloopy
and
The Wild Thang

The music below will be familiar to most of you as a mainstay of the early 60's. Although the lyrics changed, the chords stayed the same. Here is "Louie Louie", "Hang on Sloopy", and "Wild Thing."
Check it out!

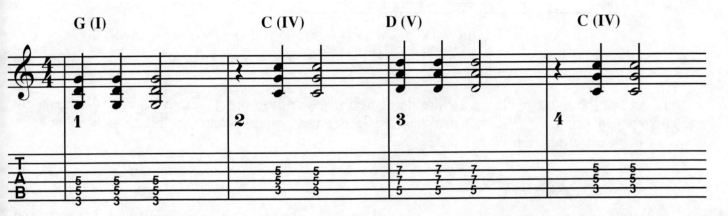

Simpler days, simpler tunes, but notice that there is a definite order to the chords that repeats over and over and over again. This order is the **chord progression**. Whether it is as simple as **Looey Sloopy** or that complex jazz chart that baffled you in your school jazz band, there are rules that progressions follow and simple ways to understand them.

Anda 1 Anda 2 Anda 1–4–5

Now in order to understand **the louie sloopy thang** on a theoretical level, we'll need to take a short look at the foundation of western music, the major scale. Let's start with a G Major scale.

Now the guitar fretboard, as we learned in **UNDERSTANDING GUITAR CHORDS**, is a unique and above all symmetrical beast. In a nutshell, this means that no matter where you start this pattern on the low E string, it will always be a **major scale.**

G Major Scale

I   ii   iii   IV   V   vi   vii   VIII (I)

Notice that the notes of this scale are numbered in ascending order. These Roman Numerals are called *degrees of the scale*. We will use these scale degrees to understand the relationships between chords and define our chord progressions.

Now look at the lowest (root) notes of *lou–sloo–thang*. The first chord is built on the 1st degree of the scale. (Let's be classy and use Roman Numerals just like real music theory people). This note always gives it's name to the I chord. Next comes the fourth degree of the scale or the IV chord and finally the fifth degree of the scale or the V chord. We have analyzed *loopy–sloopy* and determined that it is a I–IV–V chord progression.

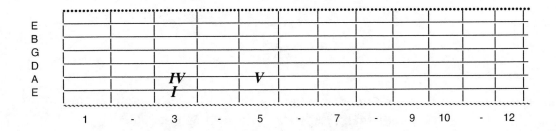

The real world intrudes

In the real world you might audition for a band and have the bass player say : "This one is easy. It's a I, IV, V progression like "Wild Thing" with a latin beat. It starts in G and goes up to B♭ by half steps. "From this cryptic conversation you would know the chords and the order that they would be played in.

Little Pickers Need Big Ears

Remember that when it comes to music it is one thing to know on an intellectual level that a chord progression is a I–IV–V but to *really* understand music you need to play and listen. Fire up that old cassette recorder or new laptop and record the part. Listen and play and learn.

Luis Luis Guitar Part

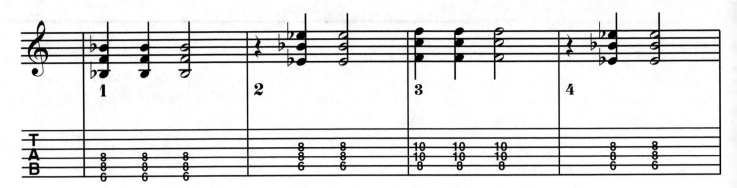

In **Luis Luis** we moved the chord progression up the neck. When we did this the pattern remains a I–IV–V while our reference point changes. If we start with G as the I chord, then the song is in the *key of G* and the chords are G–C–D. As we go up the fretboard, we change the I (and the IV and the V) and are in a new key *(Ab)* and the chords become A flat–D flat–E flat. The point is that while the chord names change, their relative positions *do not change*.

So if we look at a picture of the fretboard and locate our I, IV, and V chords we will see the following pattern.

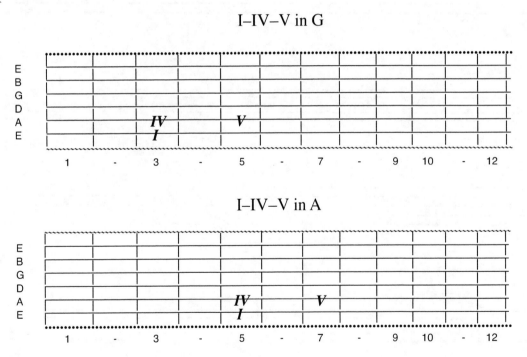

Notice that the pattern stays the same regardless of where it starts on the low E string. The fact that the patterns for chord progessions and songs keep the same relationship and shape regardless of their starting point is *The most important concept* for understanding chord progressions as a guitar player.

Punkers Delight

Loads of Punk/Metal songs are built on what I like to call the *Square of Death:*

Basic Square of Death

So now we can add a position to our *I,IV,V* fretboard grid.

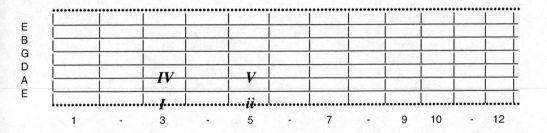

Our new position is the *ii*. This chord is built on the 2nd degree of the G major scale. Notice that the 4 root notes form a square shape on the fretboard. Using this shape to visualize a chord progression is a very useful tool. Also notice that the Roman numeral is in the lower case. This is a preview of the next chapter when we *harmonize the major scale* and find that the second chord of a harmonized scale is always a *minor chord.*

Chapter 1 Exersizes

1. On the grid below locate *I–IV and V* in the key of F major

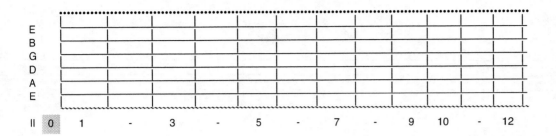

2. On the grid below locate *I–IV–V–ii* in the key of B♭ major.

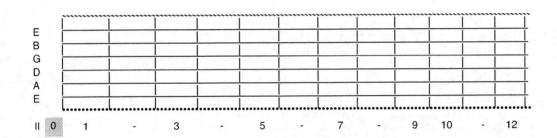

Chapter Two

Doing What Comes Naturally Harmonizing the Major Scale

Time to harmonize the C major scale below.

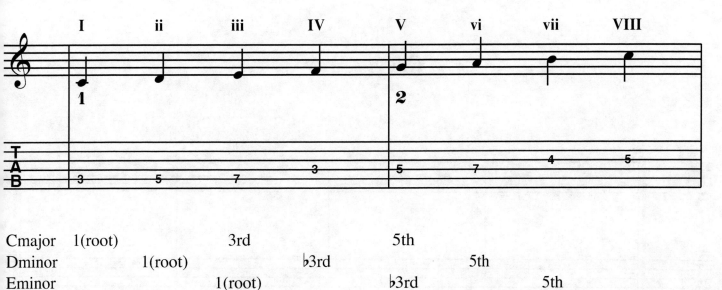

	1(root)		3rd		5th		
Cmajor	1(root)		3rd		5th		
Dminor		1(root)		♭3rd		5th	
Eminor			1(root)		♭3rd		5th

To make a C Major chord, we stack up the 3rd and 5th notes of the scale on the C to make a C–E–G triad of notes. We take the 1st, 3rd, and 5th notes of the scale or as we can see below line, line, line. Next let's do the same for D. We take the 2nd, 4th and 6th notes of the scale– D–F–A or space, space, space. This makes a D minor triad. If we continue to pile up notes for the entire major scale the result is:

The C Major Harmonized scale

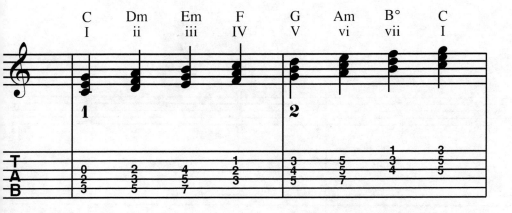

Major–minor–minor–major–major–minor–diminished (B° means B diminished) is the order of the piled up chords. Why? Don't worry about why! This is simply one those things in music that just miraculously happen. More important, it happens whenever you pile up the notes of *Any Major Scale* in this way.

Now try a little pattern using our new *harmonized triads*.

Playbreak
Reggae Way

There is no penalty for piling on

Let's go one step further and add one more note to each pile. With 3 notes, we have a 1st (root), 3rd, and 5th for each scale degree. If we add one more note we get a 1st (root), 3rd, 5th, and 7th. and the chords become–Major7 –minor7 –minor7 –major7 –dominant7 –minor7 –minor7flat5 –major7. This is the *Jazz Harmonized Scale.*

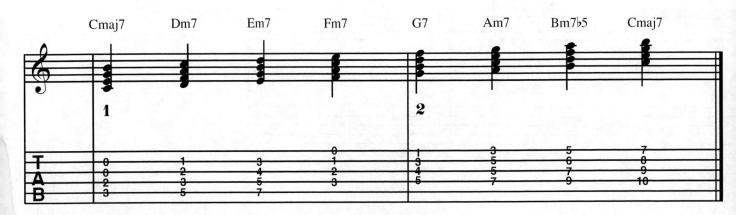

This scale in the form on the previous page is easy to play on the piano, but difficult on the guitar. The form below is much more natural to the guitar. It has the same notes as the first scale but they are in a different order.

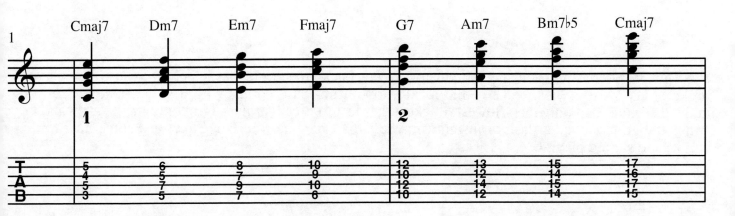

Playbreak

By harmonizing the major scale, we have created the basic chord types that will be used to build all of our chord progressions, musical forms and eventually songs. So we venture beyond our **I IV V** roots. Lets make that *Guitar* sing.

Chapter Three
We Got the Blues
The Get Down Can't Fly
whoo lawd wanna die
12 Bar Blooze

   Time for some revisionist guitar history. Way back in the old days there was a guitar player (broke as usual from visiting 12 of the local bars) sitting on a corner with a guitar. Due to lack of funds, the guitar had only the 4 lowest, thickest, hardest to break strings. With only the E, A, D and G strings the guitarist had a flash of insight (maybe the 12 bars on Bourbon Street had something to do with it) and started playing.

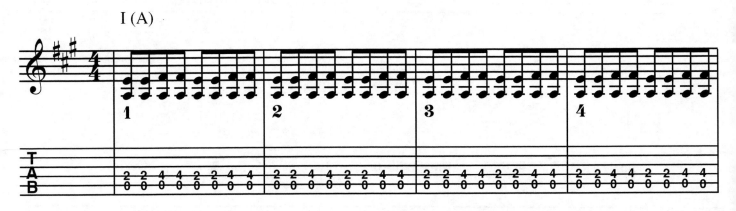

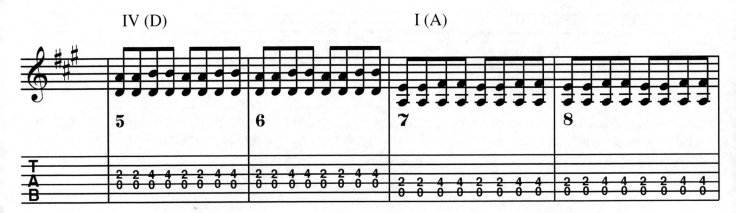

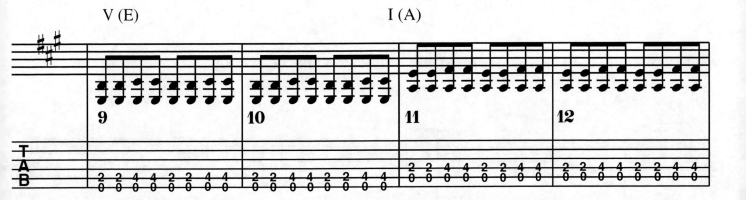

Amazingly, even with 4 strings we have our I (A), IV (D), and V (E) and can make some great music. And so the 12 Bar Blues was born (Revisionist Music History 101). Notice that we play the I chord (A) for four measures, the IV for two, back to the I chord for two more, the V for two measures and back to the I for a total of 12. This very common chord pattern is the framework for blues, jazz, rock and country. When we play this with a straight 8th note rock feel we get a Chuck Berry/Johnny B. GOODE/50's Rock feel.

Deeper Blues

With the profits from Da Basic 12 Bar Blooze our player gets a new set of 6 count'em 6 strings and takes the blues to new heights (or depths). In this next progression, we keep the basic 12 bar form with a few additions. Measures two and nine become IV chords and we add a new twist to the final two measures. Since the 12 bar form is repeated over and over we need a way to get back to the beginning. The last two measures become what is called (logically enough) a *turnaround*. This *turnaround* can take many forms, but it always has the same function. The turnaround takes us back to the beginning of the 12 bar.

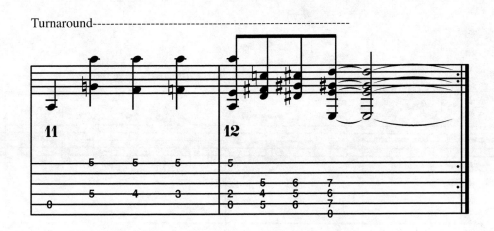

Deeper Blues

Play this one with swing 8th note feel and you're goin' to *Kansas City* baby.

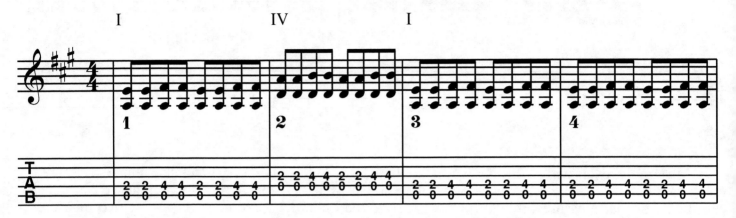

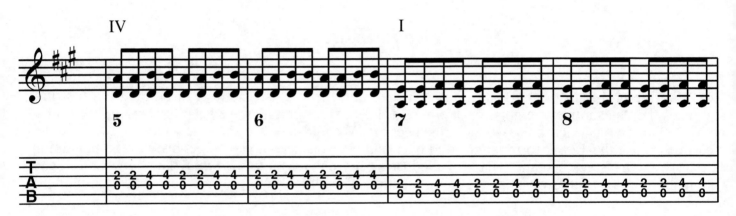

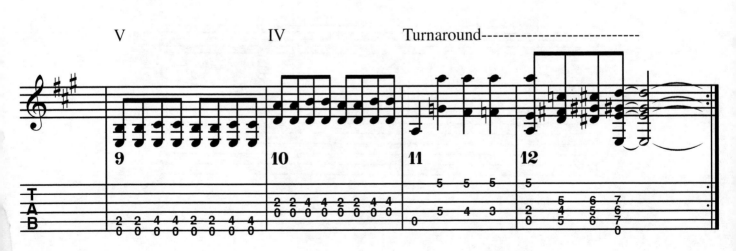

Sink or Swim (Way Deep) Blues

Next let's add to the complexity of our 12 bar. We'll have the bass (root) note follow the 12 bar pattern and suspend some new chord voicings over the root note. Notice that the three note chords (triads) are related very closely to each chord of the 12 bar. In fact, the new chords are actually similar to the chords that we used to play Looie Sloopy. Lets take a swing at *Looie goes Bloozy*. This one will take some practice.

Looie Goes Bloozy

Straight 8th note feel (notice the I–IV–V sound suspended over open A)

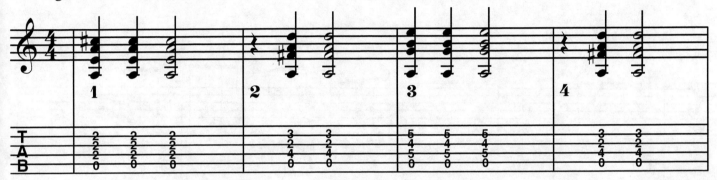

Switch to Swing 8ths feel

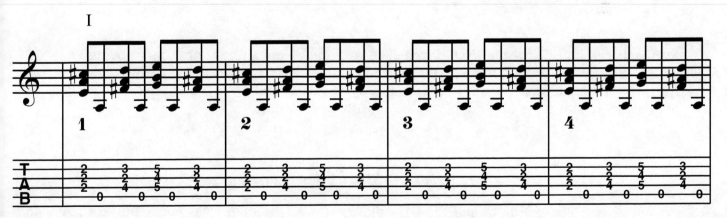

15

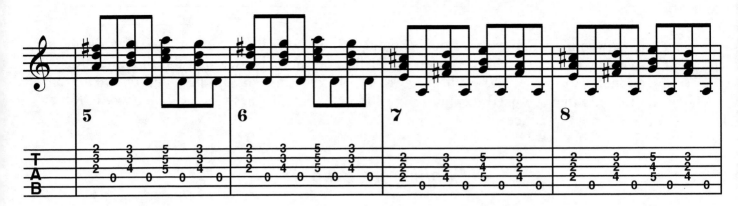

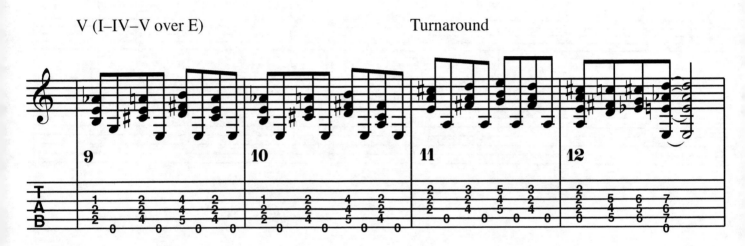

Remember to play and *listen listen listen*. The addition of substitute chords and moving voices in **Looie Goes Bloozy** gives much more texture and tension to what began as a very simple progression. But even with these additions, it still keeps it's bluesy character and drive while the *turnaround* gives it a completeness that was lacking in the raw basic form.

The real world intrudes again

So now when you audition, and the bass player sez:" This tune is a blues shuffle in A with standard turnaround. "You can say "hey okay let's play" and use chords from **Looie Goes Bloozie** to blow them away!

The Curse of the B♭ Horns

It is an unfortunate fact that there are instruments other than the guitar. This would be tolerable if trumpets, saxophones and reeds in general weren't so strange. Bad enough that these horn people think that they should always play the melody, but worse yet, they tune their instruments in a very odd manner. When you ask them to play what any fool knows is a "C", they play a B♭ or in the case of alto saxophones an E♭. Now because there are so many horns in R&B and jazz bands, most of the arrangements are written in the awful (for guitar) keys of B♭, A♭, E♭ and F major to make it easy on the **horn players**. So even though we invented the blues, guitarists get forced into these nasty keys, go figure.

Coping With the B♭ Curse

The following is a B flat major scale with the scale degree numbers marked on a fretboard grid.

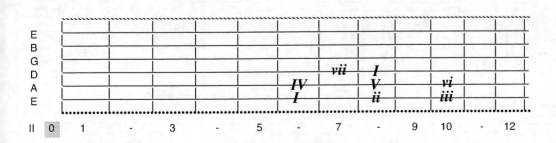

This next chord progression keeps the basic structure of the previous 12 bar forms with a few new wrinkles. First notice the use of more complex chord voicings. We will be using an E form broken shape 13th and minor 7th and C forms of the 9th an 7#9th chords

Snazzy Jazzy Blooze

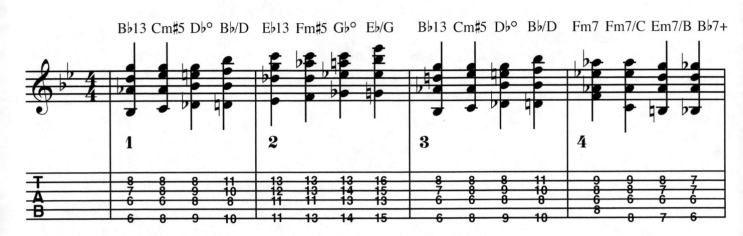

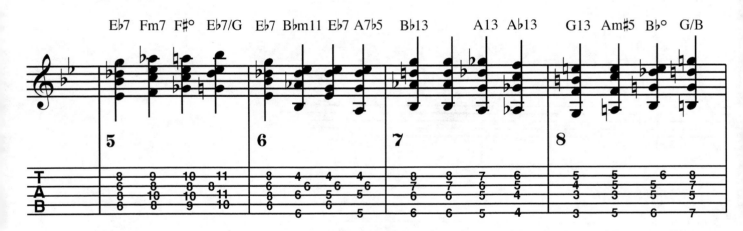

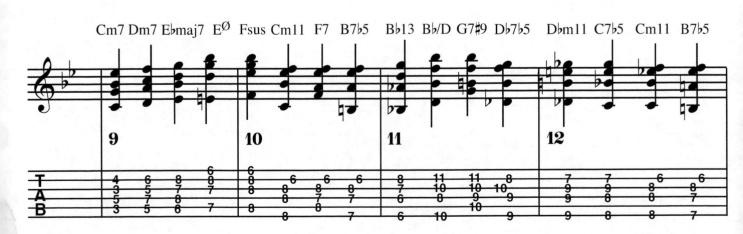

When you play this *Jazzy Blooze*, listen to the rich harmonic possibilities of each chord. When we get to the turnaround, we are adding a **VI** chord (this is called a **secondary dominant** because when we harmonized our scale, the **vi** chord was **minor or minor7**. In this case, we add the major 3rd, ♭7, and ♯9 to make this chord a Dominant family chord), and we add a **ii** (minor7) chord before the **V**. This **I–VI–ii–V** chord sequence is *VERY VERY* common and *VERY VERY VERY* important. We will see this **I–VI–ii–V TURNAROUND** over and over again. Notice also that our basic 12 bar form still underlies the progression. It is helpful to me to keep the basic form (Go, Go--Go Johny Go, Go, Go) running in my brain as a way to keep my place as we repeat the 12 bar pattern.

The bottom line is that the blues is a very flexible form. It can be very simple and rough sounding or very complex and sophisticated. If you *really* learn the blues, you will be able to communicate a very wide variety of feeling with a very wide variety of sounds.

Chapter Four

Patterns, Progressions, and Forms

So far we have talked about, played and listened to chord **PATTERNS** like *loopy sloopy I, IV, V,* and **PROGRESSIONS** like the *basic 12 bar blues*. Jazz musicians talk about playing **FORMS**. These forms are the framework of patterns and progressions that can be put together to make a song.

In the case of the 12 bar blues, the form could be as simple as playing a *melody* the *first and last* times through the progression and letting each instrument improvise for one pass through the 12 measures. More complex forms can have several chord progressions that are played in a particular order and then repeated while individual instruments play solos. Usually a set melody will be played the first time through the form. This is refered to as the *head*–as in "Let's play **Blue Monk** in B♭. I'll take the head." Grab a guitar playing friend and play the *Two Axe Blues*.

Two Axe Blues

The music below is a blues lead sheet. One guitar plays the chords above the staff and one guitar plays a melody line (**the head**) the first time through the 12 bar *form*. The next 2 times through one guitar improvises a solo. The last time through, the melody or **head** is repeated.

Two Axe Blues

Remember, solos can be as short or long as the soloist wants, but they must begin at the start of the 12 bar progression and end at the end of a 12 bar segment. The last chance for soloing is after the melody is played again. The chords to the turnaround (the last 2 measures) can be repeated as many times as the players and the soloist want to repeat them. Pay attention here as we meet this feature again in the next chapter.

A few words on soloing

Remember, the solo section can be as many 12 bar sections as the player wants to play. When you improvise a solo you are playing a melody and like any **GOOD** melody, your solo needs a beginning, an ending and a central theme. Also remember, a good solo needs to say something. Beware of playing too many notes just to prove that you can. Beware of playing the same thing too many times and finally beware of playing for too long. A too long solo can become very **BORING!** Listen to Pop songs on the radio and note the length of the solos. Generally (LED ZEP not included) solos are very short. Now listen to Jazz or Blues. There is much more room in these musical genres for soloing. In fact in Jazz and Blues, solos are what the music is all about.

Double Blue

Let's try a different feel in for the blues. Usually we associate the sound of a major chord with positive feelings and the sound of a minor chord with negative feelings.

Major = Good
Minor = Bad
Major = Happy
Minor = Sad

So if we play a blues with minor chords, it becomes even more blue than usual. To make a minor blues let's make the **I** Chord and the **IV** chord minor. The **V** chord will be a dominant chord (a 9th in this case) and in place of the **ii** chord (Aminor) we will substitute a **Tritone (E♭9th)**. We'll talk more about Tritones later. For now just play and listen.

Saint Joes Clinic

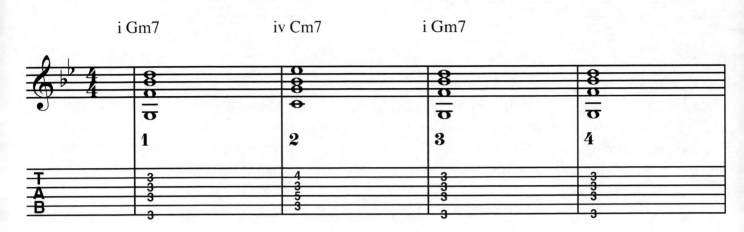

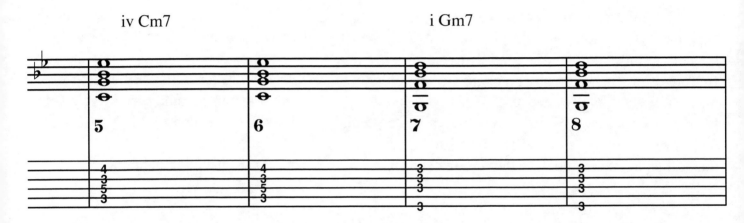

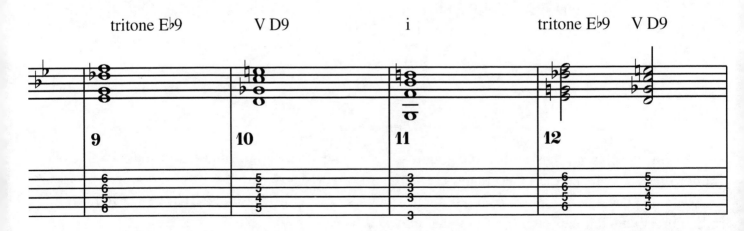

Real World Interlude

Here we are onstage at your local club at the dreaded **Jam Session**. The Jamee sez to you (the Jammer) "hey let's do a blues with a **I–VI–ii–V turnaround** in **the key B**♭ for the first tune, and tag it with the turnaround at the end. Then we'll go right into a **C minor blues**. "So, applying all that you know about the blues and all the chords you have learned you know that you **can** do it!!!

Chapter 4
Exercises

1. Write a chord chart for a 12 bar blues in the key of G major with a I–VI–ii–V turnaround.

2. Write a chord chart for a C minor blues.

Chapter Five
Turnaround And You Got Rhythm

Remember our Snazzy Jazzy and Two Axe turnarounds? A common way to end a blues is to play the turnaround (the last 2 bars) several times. During this repeated turnaround, someone (usually some tedious horn player) is bound to start soloing. Now we can see that the I–VI–ii–V chord progression is the most complex part of the blues, and that because of this it is the most challenging and ultimately the most fun place in the blues to improvise a solo.

Turnaround round round round

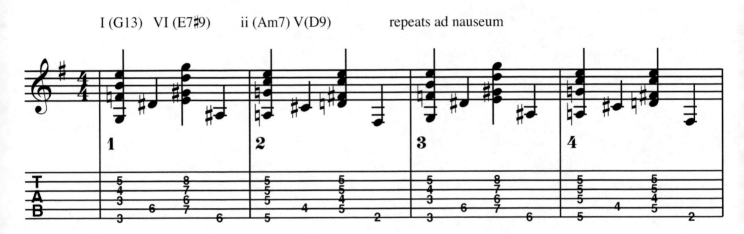

This is a nice sound but it gets just a tad **BORING** after a while! So along comes Genius George Gershwin (among others) with his ear to the blues and uses the turnaround tag (with some alterations) to create a new *form* from pieces of the blues and other stuff that was bouncing around in his ears.

The Chord Changes for the Rhythm Changes

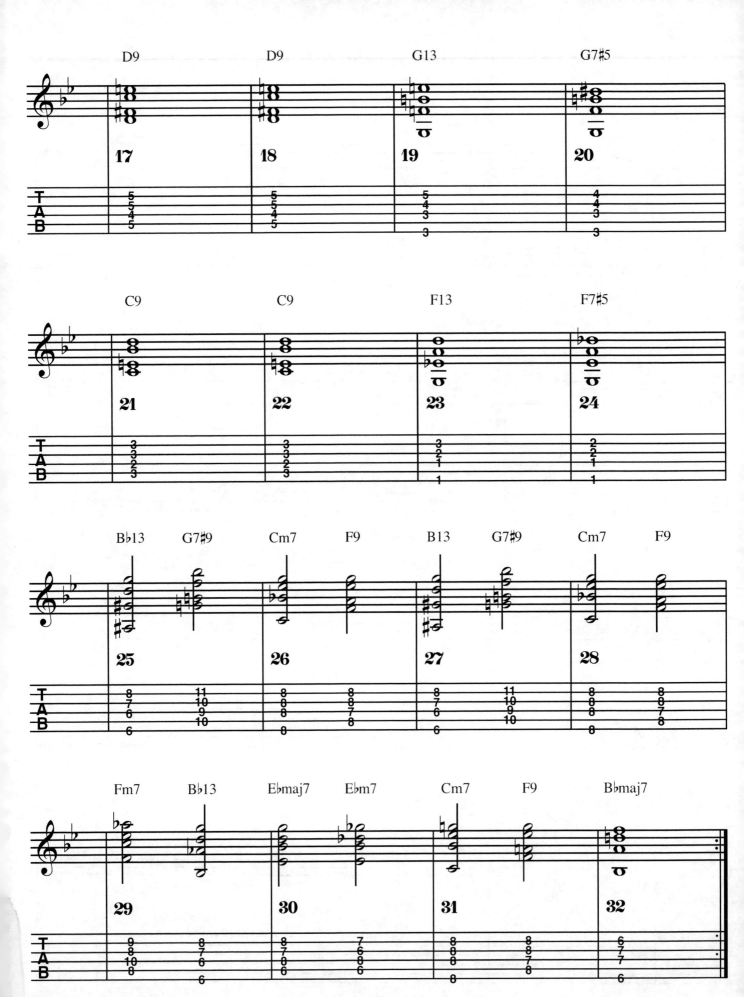

26

This chord progression is much more complex than our blues could ever be. George G's brother Ira wrote the lyrics and named it *I Got Rhythm*. Now because this is such a rich and interesting chord progression, it got used over and over (Okay, it got stolen). Musicians would write a new melody to go with the chords to *I Got Rhythm* and play improvised solos over the progression because it was very musical and very challenging. (Remember the *Flintstones Theme song?*) Eventually this progression became referred to as *I Got Rhythm chord changes* and finally just as plain old *rhythm changes*.

Before we move on, there is one more way to think about the form of a chord progression. *Rhythm Changes* is a good example of a shorthand used by jazz musicians. Look again at the chords and music to *The Chord Changes to the Rhythm Changes* on the previous page. The first 8 measures are referred to as the **A Section**. The next 8 bars are almost the same as the first 8 bars but with a different ending so this section is **A (2)**. The next 8 bars become the **B section**. Now notice that the very last 8 bars are the same as the second 8. SOOO! we play the **A section**, repeat the **A section**, play the **B section**, and play the **A section** again. The *FORM* of rhythm changes is then referred to as *AABA*.

In the real world again

Ah! we're on the beach in *JAMAICA* and the local reggae band needs a guitar player. Hey Mon! let us be jammin' on some *RIDDIM CHANGES* in B♭ major. No problem mon! Same chords as before with a new rythmic pattern.

So by combining and expanding sounds that we are already familiar with, we can create a new idea for a chord progression and form.

Chapter Six
Two Five or not ii–V
That is the Question

Notice that the chord change that has put the most variety and tension in our progressions so far is the addition of the **ii chord** (the lower case ii indicates that the chord is in minor chord family). This is true in every case from the Square of Death to the blues turnaround to Rhythm Changes. So the ii–V–I combination creates and releases tension in a way that is very natural and familiar to our ears.

One way to visualize (audialize?) the sound of these harmonic changes is to think of the AMEN at the end of a hymn.
A---ii---A---V---Men--I--

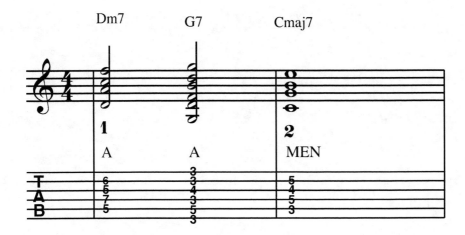

The ii–V–I chord progression is such an integral part of so many musical genres that entire pieces can be constructed using only this idea

ii–V–I/2–5–1/two–five–one

The next piece is titled **two five won**. It is a series of ii–V–I chords that take you on a trip through several keys. In it a way this chord progression is an example of the next step in the evolution of jazz forms. We swim out of the deep blues, turnaround into Rhythm Changes and let our fingers do the walking with a bunch of key changes. AMEN to that.

Two Five Won

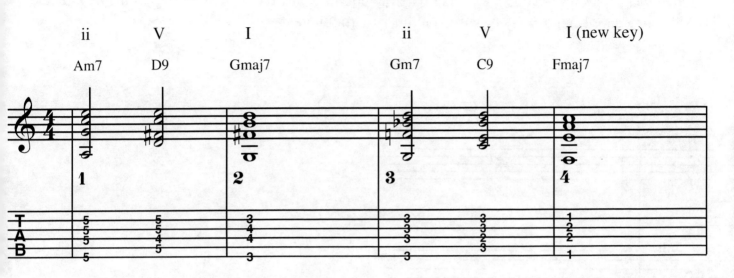

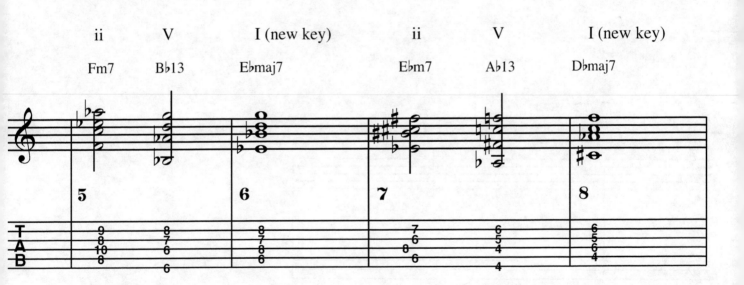

The last idea I want to get across is how and when chords can be substituted for each other in a very cool demonstration that is only available on the fret board. First, a C7 chord and next to it, a C7/G♭ which is another name for C7flat5. Just below that is a G♭7 and a G♭7♭5. You can see that the two flat5 chords have exactly the same notes, but they have different names. This is a graphic definition of the term tritone substitution. What this means is that in many cases, a G♭ chord can be *substituted* for a C chord and vice versa. The flatted 5th of any chord is refered to as the *tritone* and a substitute chord can usually be based on this new root note.

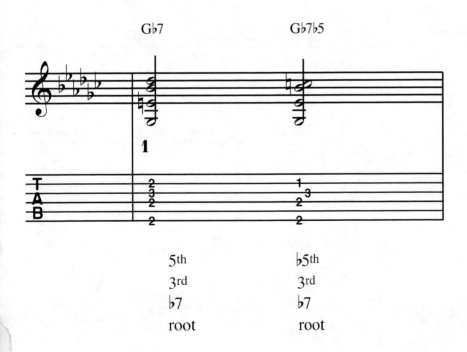

Now lets add our **TriTone substitutions** to the same changes we just played.

Two Five won the Trifecta

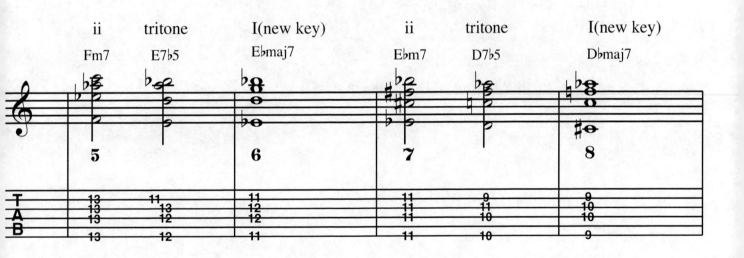

CODA

Using the ideas in this book will help you to play solos and compose better by providing a framework of how music fits on the guitar.

To sum up my way of thinking about guitar chord progressions I would like to leave you with a list of things that will improve your playing and your understanding of the guitar.

1. Learn how to build chords from the bottom up, using the basic shapes of the open E, A, D, and C major chords. (details in my book *Understanding Guitar Chords MB96932*)

2. Learn to visualize the **Shapes** of progressions. Locate the I–IV–V–ii–iii–in each key in several positions. When you are playing from lead sheets with chord symbols, try to read chords in phrases (ii–V–I) rather than individual chords.

3. Harmonize each major scale until you **know** the chords and **recognize** the sounds.

4. **Listen** to the masters of blues and jazz and then listen some more.

5. **Play!!!** Go to jam sessions, play with friends, if there is no one around record a progression and **Play with yourself**.

Good luck and have a ball. Making music is as good as it gets.